A gift for:

From:

God Thinks You're Wonderful!

A collection of encouraging thoughts from the published works of

Max Lucado

ILLUSTRATED BY CHRIS SHEA

THOMAS NELSON

Since 1798

God Thinks You're Wonderful

Published in Nashville, Tennessee, by Thomas Nelson. Thomas Nelson is a registered trademark of HarperCollins Christian Publishing, Inc.

Compiled and edited by Terri Gibbs

Editorial Supervision: Karen Hill, Administrative Editor for Max Lucado

Thomas Nelson titles may be purchased in bulk for educational, business, fund-raising, or sales promotional use. For informatiom, please email SpecialMarkets@ThomasNelson.com.

Designed by UDG DesignWorks, Sisters, Oregon.

ISBN 13: 978-1-4185-6149-9 (eBook)
ISBN 13: 978-0-8499-5650-8 (HC)

Printed in India

24 25 26 REP 43 42 41

For Jack and Marsha Countryman.
God thinks you're wonderful, and so do I.
MAX LUCADO

To my dad, Bill Givens,
with "such happiness."
CHRIS SHEA

MEMO
From: GOD
To: You
Message...
I ♥ YOU!
(and I always have...)

God is fond of you . . .

If he had a wallet,
your photo would be in it.

If found,
please return
To God
Kingdom of Heaven

I Love You!
xxoo Your son

If he had a refrigerator,

your picture would be on it.

He sends you flowers

every spring

and a sunrise

every morning.

good morning

Whenever

you want to talk,

he'll listen.

I'm always listening

He can live anywhere
in the universe,
and he chose
your heart.

X — I AM here

Face it, friend.

He's crazy about you.

By the way,

it may be difficult

for you

to believe that

God knows your name . . .

but he does.

Written on his hand.

Spoken by his mouth.

Whispered by his lips.

Your name.

The Big Book of
All MY
CHILDREN'S
NAMES
(in Alphabetical
order)
VOL I
A - Ah...

I have written your name

on my hand.

Isaiah 49:16

your name
your name
Joy
your name

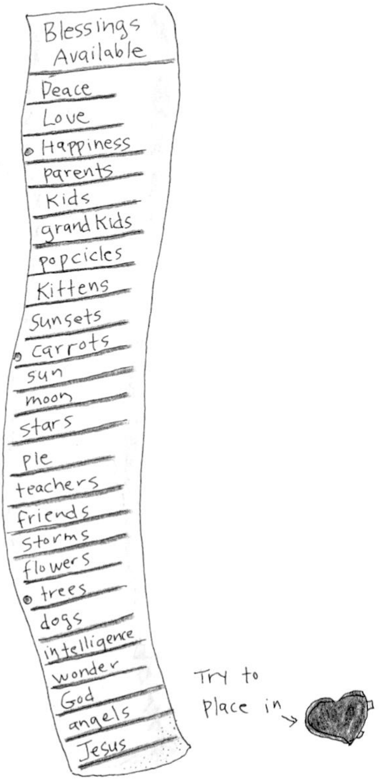
Blessings Available
Peace
Love
Happiness
parents
Kids
grand Kids
popcicles
Kittens
Sunsets
carrots
sun
moon
stars
pie
teachers
friends
storms
flowers
trees
dogs
intelligence
wonder
God
angels
Jesus
Try to
Place in

Our hearts are

not large enough

to contain the blessings

that God wants to give.

So try this.

The next time a sunrise

steals your breath . . .

or a meadow of flowers

leaves you speechless . . .

remain that way.

Say nothing and listen
as heaven whispers,
"Do you like it?
I did it just for you."

FOR YOU
Love God
Love,
MOM &
DAD

If we give gifts
to show our love,
how much more
would he?

He could have

left the world

flat and gray . . .

but he didn't.

He splashed orange
in the sunrise . . .

and cast the sky

in blue.

SKY BLUE
Heavenly Paint Co.

And if you love

to see geese

as they gather,

chances are

you'll see that too.

Best
Tail Design

Did he have to make

the squirrel's tail furry?

Was he obliged

to make the birds sing?

And the funny way

that chickens scurry . . .

BOOM
MAGNIFICENT!

or the majesty

of thunder

when it rings?

Why give a flower

fragrance?

Why give food

its taste?

Yummy!

Could it be

he loves to see

that look

upon your face?

So promise me

you'll never forget . . .

that you aren't

an accident

or an incident . . .

you are a gift

to the world,

Love
God

a divine work of art,

signed by God.

god
ORIGINAL

You knit me together

in my mother's womb.

Psalm 139:13

You were

knit together.

You weren't

mass-produced.

You aren't an

assembly-line product.

BLUE PRINT - BABY BOY
hair black
eyes brown
skin tan
heart kind
toes: 10
ORIGINAL
#4237526-BB
APPROVED
GOD

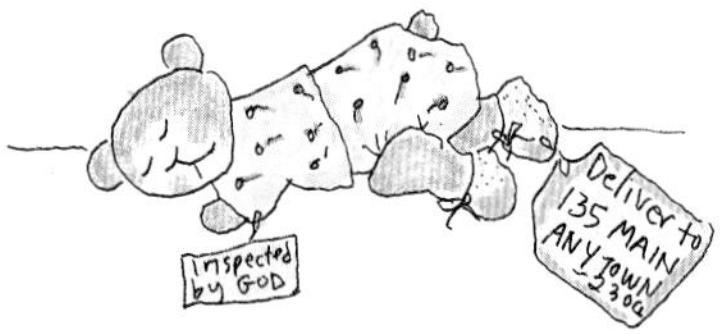
Inspected by GOD
Deliver to 135 MAIN ANYTOWN

You were

deliberately planned,

specifically gifted,

and lovingly positioned

on this earth . . .

by the

Master Crafts-Man.

Bloom here!

He thinks you are

the best thing

to come down the pike

in quite a while.

You can do it!

Turn to the sidelines;

that's God cheering

your run.

Look past the finish line;

that's God

applauding your steps.

FINISH

I Love You
xxoo
God

God is for you.

Had he a calendar,

your birthday

would be circled.

1 2 3 4 5 6
7 8 9 10 11 12 13
14 15 16 17 18 19 20
21 22 23 24 25 26 27
28 29 30 31

If he drove a car,

your name would be

on his bumper.

Your name
ALWAYS AVAILABLE
MANY MANSIONS ESTATES

If there's a tree in heaven,
he's carved your name
in the bark.

actual un-retouched photo

Maybe you don't want

to trouble God

with your hurts.

But . . .

"he cares about you"

(1 Peter 5:7).

There, there...
FIRST AID

He is waiting for you,

to embrace you

whether you

succeed or fail.

Your heavenly Father is
very fond of you
and only wants to share
his love with you.

MEMO
Blessed be
the LORD your God
who has delighted
in you. . . .
1 Kings 10:9 NKJV

Untethered by time,

God sees us all.

Vagabonds and ragamuffins all,

he saw us before we were born.

And he loves what he sees.

Flooded by emotion,

overcome by pride,

the Starmaker turns to us,

one by one, and says,

"You are my child.

I love you dearly.

I'm aware that

someday you'll turn from me

and walk away.

But I want you to know,

I've already provided

a way back."

You have captured

the heart of God.

He cannot bear to live

without you.

God's dream is

to make you right

with him.

Sins
Fault
Mistak
Love's
Eraser

And the path to the cross
tells us exactly how far
God will go to call us back.

It is not our love for God;
it is God's love for us
in sending his Son
to be the way
to take away our sins.
1 John 4:10

"Can anything make me stop loving you?" God asks.

NEVER
NO
O
NOT
IN
A
MILLION
YEARS
NEVER
EVER

"You wonder how long
my love will last?

Watch me speak your language,
sleep on your earth,
and feel your hurts.

Find your answer

on a splintered cross,

on a craggy hill.

That's how much

I love you."

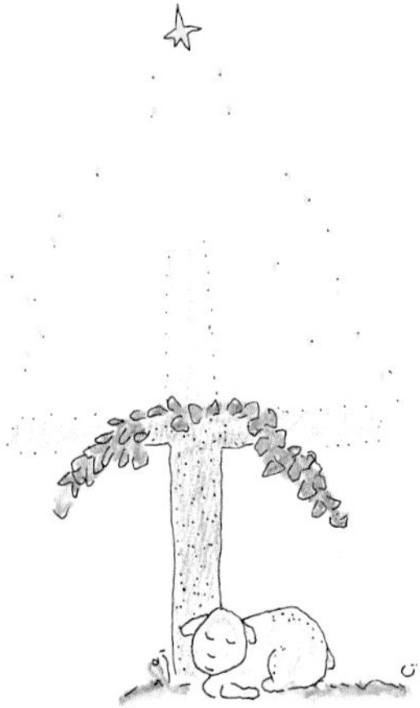

God does more
than forgive our mistakes;
he removes them!
We simply have
to take them to him.
You can talk to God
because God listens.

Let a tear appear
on your cheek, and
he is there to wipe it.

He has sent his angels
to care for you,
his Holy spirit
to dwell in you . . .

his church

to encourage you,

and his word

to guide you.

As much as you want

to see him, he wants

to see you more.

If you want
to touch God's heart,
use the name
he loves to hear.

Call him "Father."

He thinks

you're wonderful!